CW00430944

SCORPIO

The Sign of the Scorpion
October 24 – November 22

By Teresa Celsi
and Michael Yawney

MICHAEL JOSEPH · LONDON

SCORPIO

MICHAEL JOSEPH LTD

Published by the Penguin Group. 27 Wrights Lane,
London W8 5TZ

Penguin Books Ltd, Registered Offices: Harmondsworth,
Middlesex, England

First published in Great Britain 1995

Printed in Hong Kong

A CIP catalogue record for this book is available from the
British Library

ISBN 0 7181 3993 3

Contents

5

Astrology

An Introduction

Early in our history, as humankind changed from hunter-gatherers to farmers, they left the forests and moved to the plains, where they could raise plants and livestock. While they guarded their animals at night, the herders gazed up at the sky. They watched the stars circle Earth, counted the days between moons, and perceived an order in the universe.

Astrology was born as a way of finding a meaningful relationship between the movements of the heavens and the events on Earth. Astrologers believe that the celestial dance of planets affects our personalities and destinies. In order to better understand these forces, an astrologer creates a chart, which is like a snapshot of the heavens at the time of your birth. Each planet—Mercury, Venus, Mars, Jupiter, Saturn, Uranus, Neptune, and Pluto—has influence on you. So does the place of your birth.

The most important element in a chart is your sun sign, commonly known as your astrological sign. There are twelve signs of the zodiac, a belt of sky encircling Earth that is divided into twelve zones. Whichever zone the sun was in at your time of birth determines your sun sign. Your sun sign influences conscious behavior. Your moon sign influences unconscious behavior. (This book deals only with sun signs. To find your moon sign, you must look in a reference book or consult an astrologer.)

Each sign is categorized under one of the four elements: *fire*, *earth*, *air*, or *water*. Fire signs (Aries, Leo, and Sagittarius) are creative and somewhat self-centered. Earth signs (Taurus, Virgo, and Capricorn) are steady and desire material things. Air signs (Gemini, Libra, and Aquarius) are clever and intellectual.

Water signs (Cancer, Scorpio, and Pisces) are emotional and empathetic.

Each sign has one of three qualities—*cardinal*, *fixed*, or *mutable*—which shows how it operates. Cardinal signs (Aries, Cancer, Libra, and Capricorn) use their energy to lead in a direct, forceful way. Fixed signs (Taurus, Leo, Scorpio, and Aquarius) harness energy and use it to organize and consolidate. Mutable signs (Gemini, Virgo, Sagittarius, and Pisces) use energy to transform and change.

Every sign has a different combination of an element and a quality. When the positions of all the twelve planets are added to a chart, you can begin to appreciate the complexity of each individual. Astrology does not simplify people by shoving them into twelve personality boxes; rather, the details of your chart will be amazingly complex, inspiring the same awe those early herders must have felt while gazing up into the mystery of the heavens.

The Sign of the Scorpion

Scorpio, the eighth sign of the zodiac, represents sex, death, and rebirth. Both the planet Pluto, which rules this sign, and its namesake, the god Pluto of mythology, tell us much about Scorpio.

Pluto, god of the underworld, occasionally made appearances above ground, when he would open the earth and take sudden, catastrophic action, such as when he abducted Persephone and took her to his kingdom. Like Pluto, Scorpios keep their personal force under wraps, waiting behind the scenes for the right time to make a powerful, irreversible move.

The planet named after Pluto is shrouded in mystery. Long before Pluto was discovered, irregularities in the orbits of nearby planets puzzled scientists. They later found that these irregularities were caused by Pluto.

The scorpion symbol of this sign is a fascinating creature, which will sting itself to death rather than yield to a predator. Similarly, Scorpio is determined to control its own destiny at all costs.

Character and Personality

Because this naturally cautious sign tends to keep its true nature hidden, others often misunderstand the Scorpion.

Just as still waters run deep, Scorpios only reveal what they want to be seen and conceal their strong emotions beneath the surface. One reason why this sign is so secretive is that its powerful feelings leave it quite vulnerable. If the

Scorpion lets others know how deeply it feels, Scorpio fears others might use this knowledge against it.

Another reason for secrecy is that Scorpio's powerful emotions might explode if not reined in. And, when this sign has a temper tantrum, the effect can be devastating.

Like all water signs, Scorpio is concerned with emotions more than ideas, principles, or money. Being a fixed sign, Scorpio's feelings are constant. When Scorpio gives its heart, it is given completely. If a Scorpio likes you, you've got a friend for life. If not, this sign will not change its opinion easily.

Because Scorpio is so sensitive, it

stays away from things it cannot control in order to avoid pain. Even a pleasant surprise reminds Scorpio that some things are simply beyond its control. Though it may act like a loner, this sign longs for intimacy with others. However, it is careful to choose friends and lovers who will respect its privacy and feelings. In turn, Scorpio rewards intimates with intense affection and steadfast loyalty.

When wounded, however, Scorpio retaliates with a deadly sting. This sign has a long memory and will eventually repay any injury after cool deliberation. Those who cross Scorpio or betray this sign's trust will think twice before doing it again.

When Scorpio is cynical about human nature, it believes it is only being realistic. This realism is also the source of Scorpio's compassion, because the Scorpion understands how difficult life can be. If someone is truly in pain, Scorpio will find a way to help. Like Scorpio Hillary Rodham Clinton, this sign will work to make a real difference in the lives of others. However, those who are down-and-out through their own folly will never win Scorpio's sympathy. It is this sign's special gift to see through social masks and recognize people for who they really are.

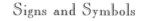

Signs and Symbols

Scorpio's ruling planet is Pluto, named for the mythical god of the underworld. Scorpio is symbolized by the Scorpion, which has a powerful sting in its tail.

A combination of the water element, which represents emotions, with the fixed quality of harnessed energy, Scorpio is both sensitive and self-possessed.

The eighth sign of the zodiac, Scorpio·

is essentially an enchanter—passionate, energetic, and possessive. Its lucky number is four.

Scorpio is associated with Tuesday. It rules the reproductive organs. Its animals include scorpions, crustaceans, reptiles, and the eagle.

The Scorpio colors are black and burgundy; the gemstones are topaz, obsidian, and sardonyx. Its metals are iron and plutonium.

Plants and flowers linked with Scorpio include heather, leeks, brambles, and blackthorn. The foods associated with this sign are onions, cayenne peppers, and all things spicy.

Health and Fitness

S corpios often take their bodies for granted and seem to enjoy pushing themselves to the limit. Their intensity and love of danger often lead them to the edge of their endurance, not realizing they have overtaxed themselves until their health breaks down.

Scorpios can rely on excellent regenerative powers, however, since this is the sign of crisis and rebirth. They benefit most from diet and rest cures, which can restore them faster than invasive procedures or strong drugs.

Though moderation is not easy for Scorpio, it is important for good health. It is much easier for Scorpio to nip potential bad habits in the bud than to try to kick them later. This is especially true of addictive substances.

Scorpio rules the reproductive organs, and those born under this sign should pay special attention to reproductive health and disease prevention.

The Scorpion loves the challenge of competitive sports and the soothing pleasure of water sports, both activities that help it stay fit.

Home and Family

The typical Scorpio is fiercely protective and demanding, with high, inflexible standards. A Scorpio parent applies this to raising children and will go to great lengths to protect its offspring from the harsh realities of life. At the same time, it teaches its children the qualities they need to survive, including good behavior, honesty, and obedience. Scorpio's offspring usually understand that their parent's high standards are worth trying to meet. And these children have the strong sense of security that comes from knowing they are deeply loved.

Love relationships are very important to Scorpio, so it will try to preserve them at great cost. As a mate, this sign is known for jealousy and possessiveness; however, Scorpio will reward devotion with deep understanding and loyalty.

Once Scorpio has found a home, it wants to stay put. A neat, orderly household is essential—if it has enough drawers, closets, and other hiding places for its treasures, this sign should be serenely happy.

Careers and Goals

Any profession that involves investigation is good for Scorpios. As doctors, they are excellent diagnosticians and surgeons. As reporters, they can smell a story a mile away.

Like all water signs, Scorpio is in tune with emotions and is especially sensitive to those in distress. As counselors, social workers, or psychologists, Scorpios can quickly zero in on underlying problems.

This sign rules banking and the professions that control other people's money. Therefore, many Scorpios choose careers in financial management fields.

Scorpios' self-discipline and loyalty make them admirable employees. Rather than seeking personal glory, they will work behind the scenes to create an efficient organization. Scorpios always try to do their jobs well and want to earn fairly the money they are paid.

To do their best work, Scorpios must respect their employers. This sign believes that accepting someone's money obliges them to be loyal, so unless they are fired, Scorpios will rarely criticize an employer.

Pastimes and Play

Those who play poker with a Scorpio soon learn they have a formidable opponent—one who knows what's in their hands, knows how to bluff, and plays for keeps.

Scorpios approach games with the same seriousness and concentration they apply to everything. They like to win, so they know all the odds and will only risk what they can afford to lose or know they can win back.

Scorpios also love to test their concentration and physical skills in sports with an element of danger, like rock climbing, race-car driving, skiing, or scuba diving.

Favorite vacation spots for Scorpions are sure to be near water. They find peace and contentment near the ocean and love to swim, especially under water.

Though Scorpios rarely indulge in gossip, they love it when people's secrets are revealed. For this reason, they are usually avid mystery readers and may secretly peek at the scandal sheets. Investigative reports of all kinds are sure to intrigue Scorpios.

Love Among the Signs

What is attraction? What is love? Throughout the centuries, science has tried and failed to come up with a satisfying explanation for the mysterious connection between two people.

For the astrologer, the answer is clear. The position of the planets at the time of your birth creates a pattern that influences you throughout your lifetime.

When your pattern meets another person's, the two of you might clash or harmonize.

Why this mysterious connection occurs can be explored only by completing charts for both individuals. But even if the chemistry is there, will it be a happy relationship? Will it last? No one can tell for certain.

Every relationship requires give-and-take, and an awareness of the sun sign relationships can help with this process. The sun sign influences conscious behavior. Does your lover catalog the items in the medicine cabinet? Chances are you have a Virgo on your hands. Do you like to spend your weekends running while your lover wants to play Scrabble? This could be an Aries–Gemini combination.

To discover more about your relationship, find out your lover's sun sign and look under the appropriate combination. You may learn things you had never even suspected.

Scorpio with Aries

(March 21– April 20)

A ries feels physically drawn to the seductive Scorpio but recoils at this sign's need for control. Scorpio admires the courage of the Ram, Aries' symbol, but retreats when the Ram gets pushy. Attraction and repulsion are equally strong for this pair. And, though they can fall deeply in love, they will always want to change each other.

Their firm loyalty to loved ones should help hold this couple together. However, some of their other similarities could provoke competition. Both are uncompromising fighters who want to win at all costs. Neither will gracefully concede a point.

Once a fight is over, Aries recovers easily and forgets about it without bearing a grudge. Scorpio will replay the argument for days—and seek revenge. With the Ram, however, Scorpio is not likely to get satisfactory vengeance; by the time Scorpio strikes, Aries will have forgotten what the offense was.

Scorpio won't understand how Aries can throw a temper tantrum and just walk away afterward. Aries will be equally mystified by Scorpio's cool exterior and its efforts to withhold its true, deep feelings. The essential difference here is Aries' apparent lack of self-control and Scorpio's extreme self-control.

Both can feel jealous, but whereas Aries will leave it at that, Scorpio will take action, accusing Aries of imagined disloyalty or keeping strict tabs on the Ram. Since Aries needs plenty of freedom, this kind of behavior will cause the Ram to rebel.

Aries is honest and shares the truth openly, which might melt Scorpio's frosty suspicions. Secretive Scorpio, however, will clam up if the Ram expects it to reveal the truth as openly and if those blunt questions become too invasive.

Both signs are passionate lovers. In the bedroom, Scorpio can appreciate Aries' emotional abandon. And the intense Scorpio sexuality is equally exciting to Aries.

To make this relationship work, both signs must give each other plenty of space. Aries must adjust to Scorpio's need for privacy, and Scorpio must give Aries enough freedom. If they can achieve this compromise, they are well on their way to a lasting relationship.

Scorpio with Taurus
(April 21–May 21)

Two pairs of eyes meet and lock in an intense gaze. The Taurus eyes are deep, inviting, and serene. The Scorpio eyes are piercing, searching, knowing. Both see in each other what they want to be, and they fall in love.

Scorpio craves the emotional security that seems so natural to Taurus, the sign of the Bull. Taurus would love to have Scorpio's penetrating mind.

This couple rarely experiences unrequited love. Either both feel an immediate, compelling attraction, or both are indifferent.

These two are intensely private signs who are exceedingly sensitive to criticism. Neither talks much. But in spite of their similarities, communication won't be that easy. Taurus needs to have everything spelled out, with no hidden meanings. So Scorpio, who communicates indirectly, must learn a new language.

Both want to control their world, but they approach this task from opposite directions. Scorpio prefers to manipulate the emotions of others, whereas Taurus works to control physical surroundings.

A sense of place and possessions provides the Bull with much of its emotional security. Scorpio's security comes from knowing that all is proceeding according to plan and that there will be no surprises.

Scorpio's tremendous drive is directed toward achieving power; Taurus's drive is toward comfort and contentment. If Scorpio tries to needle the Bull into action, rousing this placid sign from its contented mood, the Scorpion will have a formidable adversary. A raging Bull is the only sign that can consistently defeat Scorpio in battle.

This couple is an unbeatable combination in business. The Bull's tremendous endurance and Scorpio's ability to handle money, set up systems, and manage personnel make a winning team. For this reason, their household will also run efficiently.

Sexually these two are highly compatible, even super sensual, lovers, with Taurus supplying the raw, earthy energy and Scorpio the powerful imagination.

Mutual respect is the key to success for this partnership. Taurus must learn to take Scorpio seriously, and Scorpio must respect Taurus's possessions. If each can resist pushing the other too far, this couple can form a strong, lasting union.

Scorpio with Gemini
(May 22–June 21)

Serious, deep Scorpio is always surprised when it falls for a quicksilver Gemini. The sign of the Twins *seems* superficial, yet Gemini is also fascinating.

Gemini is a sign of many faces who runs on permanent fast forward. In a single day, Gemini races through a series of personality changes that can boggle the one-track Scorpio mind.

With Gemini, what you see is what you get, for that moment. Since this seems phony, even impossible, to the Scorpion, it assumes some hidden meaning lurks beneath the surface. By the time Scorpio discovers that no mystery exists, Gemini has changed again, presenting a new face and a new challenge to Scorpio.

Gemini wants to know everything and to have a wide range of experiences. Scorpio's life is much narrower but more deeply felt. The sign of the Twins is drawn to and fascinated by the Scorpion's intense feelings, which it can never completely explore.

In the casual Gemini lifestyle, everything is temporary. Gemini is always getting rid of last year's clothes, unwanted food, and boring friends. Scorpio is too emotionally attached to people and things for this and may even be alarmed by the easy way Gemini lets things go, especially if there is a chance Scorpio may be among the discards.

Honesty may be another issue with this couple. To Gemini, truth is relative and can be stretched occasionally for the sake of amusement. To Scorpio, anything other than a fact is not to be trusted.

Gemini usually has a variety of friends and can open up Scorpio's world to new people. But Scorpio may dislike the superficial small talk and gossip characteristic of Gemini's social world.

Gemini is a lighthearted lover who sees sex as a fun-filled romp; Scorpio is more passionate and intense. It may take a while for Scorpio to get used to Gemini's playful approach to lovemaking.

Gemini's fun-loving nature might be just what Scorpio needs to relax and loosen up. In turn, Gemini might blossom under Scorpio's stable guidance. When this relationship works, each partner benefits.

For this couple to survive, however, sober Scorpio and playful Gemini must both work at it. A halfhearted commitment on either side may cause Gemini to just play it for laughs, and Scorpio to cut its losses and run.

Scorpio with Cancer

(June 22–July 23)

Love at first sight happens all the time to Scorpio. With Cancer, however, there's not only love but trust at first sight.

Usually, Scorpio tends to be suspicious of everyone, especially those it loves because these are the people who have the power to hurt it most. The sign of the Crab, which protects its soft, tender inside with a hard shell, relates well to another self-protective sign and understands how to handle Scorpio's suspicions.

Both are deeply emotional water signs. These two have a strong, passionate connection and can communicate simply by gazing into each other's eyes. Their love won't need to be expressed with sweet talk since both signs can read each other's feelings at a glance.

Scorpio is proud of its ability to hide its strong emotions from most people but will find it impossible with the sensitive Crab. Cancer is the mother figure of the zodiac and has the radar to detect when loved ones are blue. Though this couple is deeply tuned in to each other, both feel the need to keep a few secrets under their shells and will constantly try to pry them out of each other. But it's useless—what the Crab and the Scorpion decide to keep secret will remain hidden.

Scorpio and Cancer will instinctively know how to please each other. Lovemaking is a very emotional experience for this pair, and their physical relations will reflect their feelings.

Both signs want security, but sometimes their concerns about money differ. Scorpio worries about acquiring money, Cancer about losing it. However, neither is a big spender, and they should be able to work out any specific financial conflicts.

Arguments will be rare for this couple. But when they do fight, their anger is usually conveyed without words. These two signs are experts in the art of the silent treatment. Both tend to retreat from each other: Cancer to nurse its wounds and Scorpio to plot revenge.

If these two signs can learn to discuss their grievances openly, they can be a very harmonious pair. With so much basic trust, which is difficult for each to find with other signs, working out any differences is ultimately rewarding for both.

Scorpio with Leo
(July 24–August 23)

Leo and Scorpio want to have their own way at all costs. If both their ways are similar, a relationship between two of the most stubborn, powerful signs of the zodiac could catch fire and accomplish great things.

But if these signs have differing goals and neither is willing to compromise, the Lion and the Scorpion could square off for battle. They have a much better chance to work out a permanent relationship if they have separate, but equal, territory—out of each other's way. Then they can be mutually supportive of each other's goals.

For this couple to get together, Scorpio may have to make the first move; Leo may be too proud to do it. If, on the first date, they can agree on the same movie or restaurant, it might be the start of a tremendously fulfilling relationship. Neither sign wants anything less than eternal devotion, but each is also willing to give it. When Scorpio and Leo fall in love, they do so with their whole hearts.

Leo's confidence is magnetic to the Scorpion, who admires anyone who can stand up to it without fear. A Lion never backs down from a fight, even against such a strong adversary as the Scorpion.

After an argument, however, Leo forgives and forgets with no hard feelings. Scorpio finds it difficult to let go of a conflict, and the urge to sting lingers. Revenge does not intimidate the Lion, though, because this sign has the confidence that it will always prevail no matter what.

This relationship often results in a career move for Scorpio, especially when the confident Leo encourages Scorpio to take a risk, such as starting a new business.

Though Leo is intensely loyal, the

Lion loves to be the center of attention and will flirt with anyone who flatters it. This could make the Scorpion feel insecure, in which case the romance could cool down fast.

Lovemaking for this pair is usually hot, with Leo's warmth and confidence bringing out the best in the passionate Scorpion. To make this relationship work, in the bedroom and out, both must make an effort always to provide the kind of attention the other sign needs so that neither will look elsewhere for love and support.

Scorpio with Virgo

(August 24–September 23)

Though Virgo and Scorpio are critical of others, they'll have few complaints about each other. These two signs are often the most trustworthy friends and understanding lovers each could hope for.

No wonder they like each other from the start: they have so much in common. Both are honest about themselves and their abilities. Neither is given to boasting or false modesty. Both like a regular, well-planned life rather than one full of surprises. They'll agree on money matters and, since both enjoy the security of a nest egg, they will not mind doing without in order to save.

Because this couple hesitates before jumping into a relationship, the momentum will probably build gradually. They often start out as pals. Virgo, not one to probe deep psychological depths, will admire Scorpio's insight. Later, sexual attraction will light a romantic spark.

Virgo's sense of how things work gives it valuable clues on how to handle Scorpio. Rather than nag or tell Scorpio what to do, the wise Virgin, symbol of

Virgo, compromises on unimportant matters and focuses on the couple's shared goals.

These two usually operate on a high-stress level. Virgo is a perfectionist; Scorpio is a control freak. However, when together, they bring each other the peace of mind and relaxation that comes from knowing that each can be trusted with responsibility.

These two are not likely to compete with each other, which helps to avoid another source of stress. Virgo will be happy to help Scorpio's dreams become realities, and the Scorpion will be eager to help Virgo reach higher goals. The only danger is that Scorpio might take

advantage of Virgo's desire to serve and ask too much of its partner. To prevent feeling exploited, Virgo should set firm boundaries on the amount of help it is prepared to provide.

Sexually, this couple should have a warm, easy relationship, with the more uninhibited Scorpio able to draw out the earthy, passionate side of the Virgin.

If both partners can avoid criticizing each other too much, this should be a very fruitful relationship on many different levels—as friends, lovers, or business associates.

Scorpio with Libra

(September 24–October 23)

Everyone loves Libra's charm. Everyone but Scorpio, that is. Though Scorpio is attracted to Libra, it isn't this sign's winning ways that draws these two together.

Perceptive Scorpio sees through Libra's smooth façade to a childlike person underneath—one who needs strong direction. Logical Libra is captivated by the strength of Scorpio's passion.

Libra loves romance but tends to be "in love with love" rather than experiencing loving feelings. Libra would like to have the bonbons and roses and skip the dramatic, operatic scenes. But Scorpio's mysterious emotional nature promises something far more thrilling than candy and flowers.

At first, Libra may not be aware of Scorpio's interest because the Scorpion rarely displays feelings with gallant gestures or lavish compliments. The attraction here is magnetic—neither will truly understand why it happened. Partly, it's the fascination of two very different types. Socially, Scorpio seems to make friends and lovers effortlessly, whereas Libra works hard at being nice to people. Scorpio wonders how someone as naive as Libra can survive in the world; Libra wonders how anyone can put up with Scorpio's stinging barbs.

Libra, the sign of the Scales, sees both sides of every issue clearly; that's why it takes so long for it to make a decision, big or small. Scorpio's absolute opinions on every subject may seem unfair to the sign of the Scales, who values compromise and may view Scorpio's inflexibility as a serious flaw.

A potential problem area is Scorpio's need for control versus Libra's need for social interaction. Though Libra's flirtations are all talk and no action, Scorpio's jealous accusations could prove to be unsettling. Finances could be another sticky issue. Thrifty Scorpio may not be interested in pursuing the more extravagant lifestyle Libra desires. Both issues should be worked out well in advance of commitment.

Sexually, Scorpio may find Libra's more romantic approach lacking, and Libra might find the emotional Scorpio too much of a good thing. But since both thrive in a committed relationship, working things out should not be difficult in the bedroom as well as in other areas of their lives.

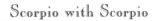

Scorpio with Scorpio

(October 24–November 22)

W hen two Scorpios fall in love, the emotional force-field is so strong that anyone within fifty yards can feel it. By the same token, when they argue, a black cloud seems to surround them.

The song "All or Nothing at All" must have been written for or by a Scorpio. They can make each other's life heaven or hell on Earth. When this pair clicks, however, they can conquer the world, like the legendary Scorpio couple Dale Evans and Roy Rogers.

Two Scorpios thinking of commitment should discuss frankly their fundamental ideas and their goals in life. Otherwise, disagreements on important issues could doom the relationship. For example, if one Scorpio wants children and the other doesn't, the one who gives in may resent the other partner. Rather than let resentment eat away at the relationship, it is far better for them to be open with each other from the beginning.

If these two do form a union, it is likely to last, since this sign dislikes short-term arrangements. Once engaged, this couple is sure to marry. All decisions with these two tend to be final, with no last-minute jitters or hesitation.

Since two Scorpios share personality traits, an instinctive understanding exists between this pair which can help them weather any emotional storms. The prime danger to this relationship is the Scorpion's tendency to get even. Each believes that he or she is right, and neither is interested in compromise. When there are disagreements, the one who gives in is tempted to get back at the other. This could be the beginning of a vicious cycle. The successful Scorpio couple will be able to rise above these harmful vendettas and to forgive each other, providing they agree on basic issues.

The love life of this couple is sacred to them and, for most Scorpio pairs, completely fulfilling. When, however, problems such as sexual dysfunction or infidelity arise, Scorpio's deep need for privacy may make it difficult to seek outside help. Therefore, it is vital for this couple to be open with each other from the start. With mutual trust, they can deal successfully with any problem that comes up.

Scorpio and Sagittarius

(November 23–December 21)

C an a sign who talks first and thinks later, like Sagittarius, get along with one who thinks first and doesn't talk at all, like Scorpio? It might not seem possible, but they do.

If these two are thrown together as coworkers or neighbors, they may develop an affection for each other as friends. But, usually, their initial attraction is hot and physical.

Both are famous for well-aimed barbs.

The difference is that Sagittarius never calculates their effects, whereas Scorpio waits for the optimum moment to strike.

The honesty of the loose-lipped sign of the Archer could blow Scorpio's cover, however, when the Archer unwittingly reveals a carefully guarded Scorpion secret. Regardless of how Scorpio might fume or take revenge, Sagittarius can't help itself; the Archer has to tell all.

Both signs want to know everything, but Scorpio will file away knowledge for later use. Sagittarius only collects information in order to share it. Scorpio likes to be the only one who knows something; Sagittarius likes to be the one who told everybody.

Appreciation of each other's finer qualities can help this couple overcome some other significant differences, such as Scorpio's need for control versus Sagittarius's need for freedom. Scorpio's intense feelings could baffle the lighthearted Archer. Sagittarius must learn to tread carefully with Scorpio, who does not take life casually and will not laugh off Sagittarius's thoughtlessness. However, Scorpio can detect that the Archer's actions are not premeditated and might be more forgiving and less vengeful with Sagittarius than with other signs.

It may take time for these two to trust each other, but when they do, their relationship will smooth out. Scorpio will understand that the free-roaming Sagittarius is not up to mischief. To keep Scorpio happy, however, Sagittarius would be wise to avoid running off every time a new adventure beckons.

Scorpio offers Sagittarius the chance for stability and accomplishment. When the Archer wants to achieve a goal, Scorpio's steadfast loyalty and unwavering support will be of great value. Though Sagittarius may have to give up some freedom and Scorpio may have to give up some control, the mutual advantages to be gained in this relationship should make these adjustments worthwhile.

Scorpio with Capricorn
(December 22–January 20)

Scorpio wants power, and Capricorn, the sign of the Goat, wants the trappings of power. These two ambitious signs could make one of the best pairs of the zodiac.

There is a strong physical and emotional attraction right from the start, though these two will be reluctant to show it. From the moment they confess their mutual attraction, however, the relationship will take off!

This couple will often find themselves discussing their goals. Both seek power for different reasons. Scorpio loves the security of being in control, whereas Capricorn loves the status that power brings. Instead of competing, these two collaborate to achieve their desires, presenting a united front to the world.

Capricorn defines itself by its work. The world of emotions is more difficult to understand and less important to this sign than the world of business. Yet the Goat is drawn to the deeply emotional Scorpion because the intensity of Scorpio's feelings is so fascinating.

In most relationships, Scorpio's secretive nature could cause friction. The Goat, however, has little curiosity, being preoccupied with moving up in the world. Unless something is really wrong, there's no use wasting time on personal details.

One might think this calculating pair would be too busy taking care of business to have time for romance, but the energy that fuels their ambitions steams up their bedroom as well. Scorpio can bring out the earthy, lusty side of Capricorn and when it does, the normally conservative Goat reacts with no holds barred!

Another big plus: Pragmatic Capricorn knows how to tone down Scorpio's intense feelings when a pleasing possessiveness turns to an irritating obsessiveness. Capricorn won't play Scorpio's emotional games and counters the Scorpion's sting with levelheaded common sense. With Capricorn, there's no wasting time over jealousy or recrimination.

Home, family, and tradition—all sacred to Capricorn—provide super-emotional Scorpio with grounding and stability. This couple takes its commitment seriously and will be able to provide a secure, caring atmosphere in which to raise a family. Together, these two signs make a team that will grow closer and more powerful as the years go by.

Scorpio with Aquarius

(January 21–February 19)

N either of these signs is really what it seems to be. Under a warm, outward manner, Aquarius, the Water Bearer, hides a cool, analytical mind. Scorpio does the reverse, hiding intense emotions under a cool façade. But there are some things these two are sure to guess about each other.

Both keep their inner selves under wraps to protect their vulnerability.

Scorpio hides its feelings rather than be exposed to possible pain. Aquarius would rather not reveal that it is uncomfortable with intimacy. The Water Bearer needs a great deal of emotional space and prefers being part of the crowd rather than getting close to any single person.

Scorpio protects itself by manipulating others and getting what it wants without their knowledge. Aquarius protects itself by relating to the crowd, even masking some individuality to fit better into the group.

To make this combination work, Scorpio will have to be much more direct with Aquarius, who dislikes any kind of scheming. And Aquarius will have to make Scorpio feel like number one, even though this may seem unfair to the rest of the world. Their basic differences are both attractive and divisive for this couple. Therefore, this will not be an easy relationship, especially since both are stubborn, fixed signs who dislike compromise.

At first, Aquarius may find Scorpio's emotional intensity sexually attractive. Once the initial infatuation is over, however, the Scorpion's all-or-nothing approach can push independent Aquarius out the door fast. Scorpio will not be happy with Aquarius's full schedule of outside activities unless the two of them share most of those same interests.

Calm discussion of financial and household responsibilities could sidestep power struggles. Otherwise, Scorpio's thrift is sure to clash with Aquarius's altruism. And Scorpio will resent being stuck at home with all the household chores while Aquarius is out saving the world.

Sexually, these two have completely different points of view. For Scorpio, lovemaking is a deep expression of emotion. For Aquarius, it is a pleasant diversion for two people in love. Aquarius is playful and experimental in bed; Scorpio is more passionate. In bed or out, these signs have much to give each other if they are willing to communicate and compromise.

Scorpio with Pisces

(February 20– March 20)

T he uniquely spiritual kind of love between Scorpio and Pisces can change their lives forever.

Like Richard Burton (Scorpio) and Elizabeth Taylor (Pisces), these two usually meet when they're involved with others. And, if they fall in love, their powerful chemistry can wipe out other commitments like a force of nature.

Though both are emotional water signs, Pisces has less fear of being hurt than Scorpio. This gives the sign of the Fish a kind of freedom Scorpio envies, though Pisces' lack of control might frighten the more conservative Scorpio. Even painful emotions wash over Pisces like ocean waves; the Fish may be tossed about, but the emotions do not last.

Being a mutable sign, Pisces is not as focused as Scorpio, a fixed sign. Therefore, the power of Scorpio's passion dazzles the changeable Pisces like an intoxicating drug. Sexually, the union can be dynamite when Pisces' fantasies ignite Scorpio's hidden desires. The chemistry between these two is strong enough to keep them fascinated for a long time.

In daily life, however, there are challenges ahead for this couple. Pisces must deal with Scorpio's jealousy and vengefulness. When hurt, the sensitive Fish swims away and rarely retaliates, but Scorpio will carry a grudge for years. Scorpio must constantly counteract Pisces' self-doubts, which often lead the Fish to self-pity and self-destructive behavior. Pisces is comfortable with clutter—too much order makes the Fish edgy. Scorpio must have order and control at all costs. Separate living quarters might be the only answer.

A strong psychic link keeps these